Cambridge Discovery Readers

Level 1

Series editor: Nicholas Tims

Vinnie's Vacation

Antoinette Moses

CAMBRIDGE
UNIVERSITY PRESS

CAMBRIDGE UNIVERSITY PRESS
Cambridge, New York, Melbourne, Madrid, Cape Town,
Singapore, São Paulo, Delhi, Mexico City

Cambridge University Press
79 Anson Road, #06-04/06, Singapore 079906

www.cambridge.org

This American English edition is based on *Harry's Holiday*,
ISBN 978-84-8323-835-6 first published by Cambridge University Press in 2011.

© Cambridge University Press 2011, 2012

First published 2011
American English edition 2012

Printed in Singapore by Tien Wah Press

ISBN 978-1-107-62130-5 Paperback American English edition

Illustrations by Mikela Prevost

Exercises by hyphen

The publishers are grateful to the following for permission
to reproduce copyright photographs and material in the publication:

Cover: Zoográfico; ©iStockphoto.com/timothyschenck; ©iStockphoto.com/artybloke
New York Red Bulls name and logo: Major League Soccer (MLS)

Contents

People in the story

Vinnie Archer: a 13-year-old boy
Mrs. Archer: Vinnie's mother
Tom: Vinnie's best friend
Zoe: Vinnie's friend
Mr. Francis: Vinnie's English teacher
Lizzie: this woman works for Your Dream Vacation
Mrs. Jackson: the principal at Vinnie's school
Peter: this man works for the New York Red Bulls soccer team

BEFORE YOU READ

1 Look at the pictures in Chapter 1. Answer the questions.

1 What is Vinnie looking at in the picture on the wall?

....

2 What do Vinnie and his mom watch on TV?

....

We're a team

"Here, Mom," said Vinnie. "Here's a cup of tea."

"Thanks, Vinnie," said his mother.

Vinnie Archer watched his mother. Her hands were bad today, he thought. He helped her take the cup. She was always bad on cold days. And this April was very cold.

"Are you OK now?" Vinnie asked. "Do you need the bathroom?"

"No, I'm fine, Vinnie," said Mrs. Archer. "Come and sit down. The soccer match is starting in five minutes."

"Yeah," said Vinnie. "And it's a big game. The New York Red Bulls against LA Galaxy. I can't wait!"

Mrs. Archer laughed. "You're just like your dad. When you were a baby, your first word . . ."

". . . was soccer," said Vinnie. "I know, Mom!"

"Your dad laughed and laughed." His mother smiled. Vinnie smiled too.

He thought about his father. "Do you think Dad is watching this game?" he asked.

"Of course he is. He's a Red Bulls fan[1], like you," his mom replied. "He always watches his favorite team."

"Where is he today?" Vinnie asked. He looked at the picture on the wall of his dad next to a ship.

"Brazil," said his mother. "They're leaving on the ship today."

"Hmm," thought Vinnie. He looked out of the window. "It isn't cold in Brazil."

"He's going to be home for Christmas this year," his mother told him.

"That's great," said Vinnie. "It isn't easy without Dad."

"No," replied his mother. "It's hard for you. But I can't . . ." She stopped and looked down at her hands.

"It's all right, Mom," said Vinnie quickly. "We're fine, you and me."

"But it isn't all right," she replied. "You don't do the things that other teenagers do."

"They don't do anything interesting," said Vinnie.

"But other teenagers play soccer, talk to their friends, go shopping, and other things. You're always at home. It's Saturday today, there's a big game, and you're here watching it with me."

"It's OK," said Vinnie. "I don't need a ticket to the game. It's a lot of money."

"I know," said his mom. "Perhaps you can stop eating chocolate for a month to get the money for a ticket?"

Vinnie laughed. "I don't know, Mom . . . a month is a long time!"

"I know it's hard for you," said his mom. "But when my arthritis is bad, I can't do anything."

"And that's why Mrs. Stevens comes here," said Vinnie.

"Yes," said his mom. "Mrs. Stevens cleans the kitchen and the bathroom, but she doesn't buy food or cook. You do all that. And you do everything on the weekends."

"Mom, it's all right," said Vinnie. "We're OK, you and me. We're a team."

"Yes, but I often think about all the things you can't do," his mom replied. "You can't play soccer after school. You can't go to the movies. You can't –"

"Shh, Mom," said Vinnie. "The game is starting . . ."

Twenty minutes later, Galaxy got a goal. Red Bulls 0, Galaxy 1.

"One goal is OK," said his mother. "The Red Bulls are going to win this game. I know it."

She looked over at Vinnie. His eyes were almost closed. He was tired.

LOOKING BACK

●●

1 Check your answers to *Before you read* on page 4.

ACTIVITIES

●●

2 Complete the sentences with the names in the box.

> Vinnie's dad (x2)   Vinnie (x3)
>
> Vinnie's mom (x2)   Mrs. Stevens

1 ..... *Vinnie* ..... gives his mom a cup of tea.

2 .... is never good when it's cold.

3 The first word .... said was *soccer*.

4 .... is on a ship in Brazil.

5 .... is going to be home at Christmas.

6 .... can't do anything when her arthritis is bad.

7 .... comes to the house to clean.

8 .... is very tired.

3 Underline the correct words in each sentence.

1 Vinnie helps his mom take the cup of <u>tea</u> / *coffee*.

2 The soccer game on TV is starting in *five* / *ten* minutes.

3 The Red Bulls are playing *Brazil* / *Galaxy*.

4 There is a picture of Vinnie's dad next to a *car* / *ship*.

5 Vinnie is at home with his *mom* / *dad* on Saturday.

6 Vinnie says other teenagers *do* / *don't do* interesting things.

7 Mrs. Stevens cleans the *bedrooms* / *kitchen*.

4 Who or what do the <u>underlined</u> words refer to?

> Vinnie's dad   a ticket to the game   ~~Vinnie's mom~~
>
> Vinnie (x2)   Mrs. Stevens   Vinnie and Vinnie's mom

1   He helped <u>her</u> take the cup. (page 5) _Vinnie's mom_

2   "<u>You</u>'re just like your dad." (page 6) ....

3   "<u>He</u>'s a Red Bulls fan." (page 7) ....

4   <u>She</u> doesn't buy food or cook. (page 8) ....

5   "<u>It</u>'s a lot of money." (page 8) ....

6   "<u>We</u>'re a team." (page 9) ....

7   <u>He</u> was tired. (page 9) ....

5 Match the questions with the answers.

1   What are Vinnie and his mom going to watch on TV? [a]

2   What is Vinnie's and his dad's favorite soccer team? ☐

3   When is Vinnie's dad going to be home? ☐

4   Who buys and cooks the food? ☐

~~a~~   Soccer.

b   Vinnie.

c   The Red Bulls.

d   Christmas.

LOOKING FORWARD
• •

6 Check (✓) what you think happens in Chapters 2 and 3.

1   Vinnie wants to win a vacation for his mom and dad. ☐

2   Vinnie plays soccer after school and doesn't look after[2] his mom. ☐

Chapter 2

The contest

It was Wednesday morning, and Vinnie and his best friend, Tom, were in their classroom.

"And Vinnie Archer runs up to the ball, and he kicks it and –" Tom shouted.

As Vinnie kicked the ball to Tom, their English teacher, Mr. Francis, walked in and caught it.

"All right, Mr. Francis," said Tom.

"No balls in the classroom, Vinnie," said Mr. Francis. "You know that."

"Sorry, Mr. Francis," said Vinnie.

"You can play during the break, lunchtime, and after school," said Mr. Francis, "but not in the classroom."

"Vinnie never plays soccer after school," said Zoe, and laughed.

Vinnie's face went red. Everyone in the class knew that he was different[3]. He went home after school and didn't play with them, or go out. But only Tom knew the reason. He didn't want everyone else to know.

"Shh!" Tom told Zoe.

After class, Zoe went up to Vinnie and said sorry. Vinnie knew that Zoe's family had problems too. Her family lived on Vinnie's street. He sometimes saw a police car in front of their house.

"That's OK, Zoe," said Vinnie.

"I've got a soccer magazine," said Zoe. "It's my brother's. Do you want to read it?" She gave it to Vinnie.

"Hey, thanks, Zoe," said Vinnie, and he took the magazine.

Zoe liked Vinnie. He had a nice smile. He was smiling now, with the magazine in his hand. Zoe smiled too and left the room.

"Zoe likes you," laughed Tom.

"Don't be stupid," said Vinnie.

Tom took the magazine. "Look, there's a picture of the Red Bulls here." Then he stopped.

"Hey, Vinnie," he said. "Look at this ad. It's a contest[4]. It says that you can win a vacation to Florida and it's easy. You never go on vacation."

Vinnie didn't reply.

"We're going to go to Ocean City this year," said Tom. "My uncle's got a hotel there. They've got lots of rooms at the hotel. I can talk to Dad. You can come too."

"I can't," said Vinnie. "I can't leave Mom."

"Oh, yeah," said Tom. "Sorry. You can't leave your mom, but . . . she can go to Florida! With you!"

"Hot weather is good for people with arthritis," said Vinnie.

"So you have to win this vacation," said Tom.

Vinnie looked at the ad.

"Write 500 words about why you want a vacation," he read, "and send it to Your Dream^5 Vacation."

"You're good at writing stories," said Tom.

Vinnie smiled. "I'm going to do it. I'm going to win the vacation. We can all go to Florida. Mom and Dad are going to sit in the sun, and we're all going to have a vacation!"

Chapter 3

Five hundred words

The next day Vinnie told his friends about the contest.

"I'm going to write 500 words," he said.

A boy named Sam laughed. "I know 500 words," he said.

"Yes," said Tom, "and they're all bad words!"

Everyone laughed.

"Why do you want to win a vacation, Vinnie?" Zoe asked. Vinnie opened his mouth. He wanted to say, "The vacation is for my mom," but he didn't.

"That's the contest question," said Tom.

"Yes," said Vinnie quickly.

"How do you win?" Zoe asked.

"I write 500 words and say why I want this vacation," said Vinnie. He stopped and thought.

"Why do you want to win?" Zoe asked again.

"I want to go to Florida because . . ." He stopped again. He didn't want to tell his friends about his mom.

"I want to go to Florida because it's raining today," said Zoe.

"I want to go to Florida because we have Math today," said Sam.

"I want to go to Florida because it's a free[6] vacation!" said Tom.

"Great," said Vinnie, and he laughed. "Thanks everyone."

That evening, Vinnie sat in his room at home and started writing:

I want to win this vacation because I never go on vacation. My dad works on a ship, and my mom has arthritis. After school, I look after her and …

Vinnie stopped and read the first sentences again. "This is boring," he thought. He started again.

In a small room in an apartment in New York sits a woman. She doesn't want to sit in this apartment. She wants to do things. She likes music and dancing. She loves cooking for her family. But she doesn't do these things because she has arthritis. Her hands and feet and legs often hurt[7]. But she never talks about it.

This woman is my mother. She smiles all the time, but nothing is easy for her. I want her to laugh. I want her to have fun. And a vacation can do this for her.

You can get arthritis at any age. More than 50 million people in the United States have it. Some are like my mom, and it's very bad. They feel tired all the time. Their arms, legs, or hands hurt a lot. It never stops. Some days it's bad. On other days it's very bad.

"This is good," thought Vinnie. But he also wanted to write about his mother before the arthritis. She worked in an office[8] then, and she loved dancing. She smiled a lot. She was happy.

"Can I do this?" he thought. "Can I win this vacation?" Vinnie starting writing again.

LOOKING BACK

1 Check your answers to *Looking forward* on page 11.

ACTIVITIES

2 <u>Underline</u> the correct words in each sentence.

1 <u>*Zoe*</u> / *Tom* says that Vinnie never plays soccer after school.

2 Vinnie sometimes sees a *bus* / *police car* in front of Zoe's house.

3 There's a picture of *Galaxy* / *the Red Bulls* in the soccer magazine.

4 Tom is going to *Florida* / *Ocean City* for his vacation this year.

5 *Sam* / *Tom* says he wants to go to Florida because it's a free vacation.

6 Vinnie writes 500 words *at school* / *at home* for the contest.

7 Vinnie's mom loved *dancing* / *running* before the arthritis.

3 Put the sentences in order.

1 Zoe says she's sorry to Vinnie after class. ☐

2 Mr. Francis catches the ball. ☐1☐

3 Tom sees the vacation contest in the magazine. ☐

4 Vinnie starts writing 500 words for the contest. ☐

5 Zoe gives Vinnie a soccer magazine. ☐

6 Tom says Zoe likes Vinnie. ☐

7 Vinnie tells Zoe and Sam about the contest. ☐

4 Are the sentences true (*T*) or false (*F*)?

1 Mr. Francis says Vinnie and Tom can play soccer in the classroom. $\boxed{F}$

2 Vinnie knows that Zoe's family have problems too. ☐

3 Zoe thinks Vinnie has a nice smile. ☐

4 Vinnie can go to Ocean City with Tom. ☐

5 Tom says Vinnie is good at writing stories. ☐

6 Vinnie is going to write 400 words for the contest. ☐

7 More than 50 million people in the United States have arthritis. ☐

8 Before the arthritis, Vinnie's mom worked in a store. ☐

5 Answer the questions.

1 Why does Vinnie never play soccer after school?

....

2 Where does Tom's uncle have a hotel?

....

3 Why does Vinnie write 500 words?

....

LOOKING FORWARD

6 Check (✓) what you think happens in Chapters 4 and 5.

1 Vinnie's mom doesn't want a vacation to Florida. ☐

2 Vinnie gets a letter from Your Dream Vacation. ☐

Chapter 4

Vinnie won!

The next day, Vinnie sent his letter to Your Dream Vacation. For two months, he heard nothing about the contest. There was a week's vacation from school. The Red Bulls lost four games in May. Teachers started talking about the end-of-year exams.

Then, one day in June, Vinnie got a letter. He ran into the kitchen with it.

"Mom!" shouted Vinnie, "I got a letter. It's from Your Dream Vacation. It's about the contest!"

"What contest?" asked his mother.

"It was a contest to win a vacation to Florida," said Vinnie.

"You didn't tell me about that!" said his mother. "Did you win?"

Vinnie opened the letter and smiled. "Yes, I won!"

"Wow!" said Vinnie's mom. "What does it say?"

Vinnie gave her the letter and she read it. "This is great, Vinnie," she said. "But you can't go without Dad or me."

"I know, Mom," said Vinnie. "I wanted to win the vacation for us – for you, me . . . and Dad, if he can come."

"Oh, Vinnie," said his mom.

"And the vacation is free," said Vinnie. "We can sit in the sun, and you can feel good again."

"Thank you so much, Vinnie," said his mother. "I have to tell your dad. He's going to be very happy."

Vinnie ran to school.

"I won the contest!" he told Tom.

"Contest?" his friend replied.

"The vacation!" Vinnie shouted. "To Florida!"

"Wow!" said Tom. He got onto his chair and shouted, "Vinnie won!"

Mr. Francis walked in and stopped.

"What are you doing, Tom?" he asked.

"Sorry, Mr. Francis," Tom said. He got off the chair. "Vinnie won a free vacation. In a contest," said Tom.

"Is this true?" asked Mr. Francis.

"Yes," said Vinnie. He told Mr. Francis all about the contest. "I wrote 500 words," he said. "It was like an essay."

"Wow, Vinnie," said Mr. Francis, smiling. "You have to read it to the class. We want to hear it."

Vinnie had a copy of his contest essay in his backpack, but he didn't want to read it to the class. He didn't want to tell everyone about his mom.

"I don't have it here," Vinnie replied. "It's at home."

After class, Vinnie walked over to Mr. Francis's desk. He wanted to talk to him about his essay. He liked Mr. Francis. "He's going to understand," thought Vinnie.

"Mr. Francis," Vinnie said. "I don't want to read my contest essay to the class."

"Why?" asked Mr. Francis.

Vinnie took the essay out of his backpack and gave it to his teacher. Mr. Francis read about Vinnie's mother and her arthritis, and about the work that Vinnie does for her every day.

"I understand now, Vinnie," said Mr. Francis. "It's a very good essay."

"Thank you," said Vinnie, and gave him the letter from Your Dream Vacation.

"I need to go to this hotel in New York on June 10th. I need to get the tickets," he told Mr. Francis. "It's downtown[9].

But June 10th is a Friday. It's a school day."

"Oh," said Mr. Francis.

"Can I go?" Vinnie asked him.

"I can ask the principal, Vinnie," Mr. Francis said, "and you also have to ask your mother."

* * *

On June 10th, it was sunny. Vinnie got up very early, dressed, and had his breakfast.

"Good luck," said his mom. She looked at her watch. "You need to go. You're going to be late!" She smiled at Vinnie, and he left the apartment.

Vinnie walked to the 96th Street subway station near his apartment. He took the subway to Times Square and walked to the hotel. It was a big hotel, and there were lots of people there. Vinnie spoke to the woman behind the desk.

"Hello. I'm here for the Your Dream Vacation contest," he said.

"They're in the room over there on the left," she replied.

Vinnie opened the door. The room was full of people. "There are a hundred people in this room," thought Vinnie. "Why are all these people here? Did they all win a vacation like me?"

Chapter 5

We all won!

Vinnie stood at the back of the room. There was a woman near him, and he went up to her.

"Excuse me," he said. "Is this the room for Your Dream Vacation?"

"Yes," she replied. "Did you win?"

"Yes," said Vinnie.

"I'm a winner¹⁰ too," she said. "Everyone here is a winner."

"I don't understand," said Vinnie.

"Come and sit down," said the woman. "They're going to tell us everything."

Vinnie sat down. "There are a hundred people in the room," he thought. "But a hundred free vacations is a lot of money. Why are there lots of winners?"

Then a door opened and a woman with a big smile walked into the room.

"Hello everybody," she said. "My name is Lizzie, and I work for Your Dream Vacation. You're here today because you are all winners. Yes, you're all winners of a dream vacation to Florida!"

"Hooray!" shouted a man. Everybody laughed.

"This is great," thought Vinnie. "We're all going to get a free vacation."

"Now," said Lizzie. "This is your hotel." There was a picture behind her. It was of a very big hotel. "It's next to the ocean and it has 300 rooms," Lizzie told them. "It also has two swimming pools and a large garden."

Vinnie thought about him and his mother in the hotel. "Mom loves flowers. She's going to love the hotel's garden," he thought. "And she can sit next to the swimming pool and read."

"It's a beautiful hotel," said Lizzie. "And all the food and drinks are free. You can eat and drink all day!"

"It looks great," Vinnie said to the woman next to him.

"Yes," she said, happily.

"Yes, it looks great, but is it all true?" said the man next to her.

"This is my husband," said the woman. "He doesn't think the vacation is going to be free," she told Vinnie.

"They tell us that the food and drinks are free," said the man. "But what about the other things?"

Lizzie smiled at everyone.

"Isn't it a beautiful hotel?" she said. "It's very new. And we fly you to Florida from any New York airport for free."

"Excuse me," the man said. He stood up. "Is the hotel free?" he asked Lizzie.

Lizzie smiled. "Well, we can't give everyone a week at a very expensive hotel." She laughed. "But we fly you to Florida, and we pay[11] for all your meals and drinks at the hotel."

"And the hotel?" the man asked again.

"Yes, you need to pay for the hotel," said Lizzie very quickly. "Of course you pay for the hotel."

Then a woman at the front spoke. "How much is it?" she asked.

"It isn't very expensive," said Lizzie. "There's a special price, just for winners of this contest."

"We pay for the hotel?" said the woman next to Vinnie. She didn't look happy now.

"It *looks* like an expensive hotel," said her husband. He stood up. "It isn't a free vacation. This isn't a dream vacation," he shouted at Lizzie. "It's a *bad* dream!"

LOOKING BACK

. . . .

1 Check your answers to *Looking forward* on page 21.

ACTIVITIES

. . . .

2 <u>Underline</u> the correct words in each sentence.

1 The Red Bulls *won / lost* four games in May.

2 The letter from Your Dream Vacation says Vinnie
won / didn't win the contest.

3 At school, Vinnie has his contest essay in his
jacket / backpack.

4 Vinnie goes to a hotel in *New York / Ocean City* to get
the vacation tickets.

5 Vinnie takes the subway to *96th Street / Times Square*.

6 Lizzie says the *hotel / food* is free.

3 Complete the sentences with the words in the box.

garden	June 10th	Lizzie
~~for two months~~	chair	essay

1 Vinnie doesn't hear about the contest *for two months* .

2 Tom stands on a .... and shouts "Vinnie won!"

3 Mr. Francis says Vinnie's .... is very good.

4 Vinnie needs to go to a hotel on ....

5 .... works for Your Dream Vacation.

6 The hotel has a ....

4 **Match the two parts of the sentences.**

1 What does Vinnie's letter from Your Dream Vacation say? $\boxed{b}$
2 Why doesn't Vinnie want to read his essay to the class? ☐
3 Why does Vinnie take the subway on June 10th? ☐
4 Why are all the people at the hotel? ☐
5 Why doesn't the woman next to Vinnie look happy? ☐

a Because he goes to a hotel downtown to get the tickets.
b̶ He won the contest.
c Because they're all winners.
d Because she must pay for the hotel.
e Because he doesn't want to tell everyone about his mom.

5 **Answer the questions.**

1 Why does Vinnie run into the kitchen?

....

2 What does Vinnie need to ask his mother?

....

3 What is going to be free at the hotel in Florida?

....

4 Why does the man shout at Lizzie?

....

LOOKING FORWARD
• •

6 **Check (✓) what you think happens in the last three chapters.**

1 Vinnie's dad comes home. ☐
2 Vinnie's mom gets a new caregiver[12]. ☐

Chapter 6

A bad dream

"This *is* a bad dream," thought Vinnie. He sat in the chair in the hotel room. His mom and dad didn't have money for an expensive hotel.

He left the hotel and walked back to the station. "I'm not a winner," he thought. "I didn't win anything."

Vinnie walked into the apartment, and his mother knew that something was wrong.

"What is it?" she asked.

"I didn't win a free vacation," said Vinnie. "They don't pay for the hotel." He told his mother about Lizzie and Your Dream Vacation.

"I'm sorry, Vinnie," she said. "Your Dream Vacation just used the contest to tell people about the hotel. I'm very sorry," she said again.

"What am I going to tell everyone at school?" asked Vinnie. "They think I won a vacation."

"Tell them everything," said his mother.

"But I can't tell them why I wanted the vacation," said Vinnie. "I can't tell them about you and the arthritis and everything."

"Your friends don't know about me?" asked his mother.

"They know I need to help at home a lot," said Vinnie. "They know you aren't always well. But they don't know why. Tom knows, but the others don't."

"Then you're going to tell them," said his mother. "You look after me every day, and your friends need to know about it."

Vinnie didn't say anything.

"Look, Vinnie," said his mom. "We're a great family. I love your dad and he loves me. He's got a good job, and you're a great son. Your dad and I love you. Think about Zoe and her family. Zoe's mother comes to see me sometimes. They've got a lot of problems."

At school on Monday, Vinnie told the class about Your Dream Vacation. But he didn't tell them about his mom.

"That isn't right," said Tom. "So they take you to Florida, but you pay for the hotel?"

"Yes," said Vinnie.

"I'm sorry, Vinnie," said Mr. Francis.

"It isn't right," said Tom again. "It isn't fair."

Vinnie's friends were all angry. "You have to tell people about this," said a boy named David.

"Yeah," said a girl. "Write about it, Vinnie."

"That's a good idea," said Tom. "You can write about the contest on the school Web site. Then everyone in the world can read about it!"

"I don't know," said Vinnie.

"I can write about it," said Tom. "Can I?" he asked Mr. Francis.

"Ask Vinnie," said Mr. Francis.

Vinnie thought about his mom. She wanted his friends to know everything.

"Yes," said Vinnie. "Write about my mom. You can tell people why she needs a vacation."

"Are you sure? Do you want Tom to write about it?" asked Mr. Francis.

"Yes, I'm sure," said Vinnie. He looked at the other students in the room. "I know you all think I'm stupid because I'm always at home and I never go out after school. But my mom's sick. She's got arthritis and I look after her. I'm not stupid. I'm a caregiver."

"Thank you, Vinnie," said Mr. Francis. "I think we all understand that it isn't easy to tell us about your mother.

Being a caregiver is not easy. And you aren't stupid. We all know that."

"Yeah," said Zoe. She smiled at Vinnie, and he smiled back at her.

"It's Your Dream Vacation that is stupid," said Tom. "But now everyone is going to know about them!"

Chapter 7

The school Web site

That night, Tom wrote about Vinnie and his mother. He worked for over two hours. In the morning, he asked Vinnie to read it first. Vinnie liked it. Tom wrote well.

Then, in the afternoon, Tom saw Vinnie again.
"Fifty people visited the school Web site today!" he said.
The day after, they looked again. It was 400 people.
The day after that it was 2,000.

A week later, Mr. Francis came into class and asked Vinnie to come to the office of the principal, Mrs. Jackson.

"Is it bad?" asked Vinnie.

"No," said Mr. Francis. "Actually, it's very good. But Mrs. Jackson's going to tell you everything."

They went into the office. Mrs. Jackson smiled at Vinnie.

"Hello, Vinnie," she said. "Do you see all this paper?"

Vinnie saw a lot of paper on Mrs. Jackson's desk.

"Yes," he said.

"These are all e-mails for you," she told him.

"Oh," said Vinnie. "I'm sorry."

"It's all right," she said and smiled. "But you have a lot of work to do. You must reply to all of them."

Mrs. Jackson gave him one of the e-mails. It was from a girl in England.

"Hi, Vinnie," he read. "My name is Lisa and I'm a caregiver too. My parents can't see, and I do everything for them before and after school."

He stopped reading and looked at Mrs. Jackson.

"There are lots of e-mails like this," said Mrs. Jackson. "And there are letters too."

She gave him a letter, and he opened it. "Dear Vinnie," the letter said. "We are an organization[13] called Young Caregivers, and we read about you and your mother on your school Web site. We want you to write something for our Web site about your life as a young caregiver. We also have vacations for young caregivers, and we want to give you a vacation this summer."

"Young Caregivers wants to give me a vacation," Vinnie told Mrs. Jackson. "But what about my mom?" he asked her.

"Now that everyone knows about your mother, things are going to change," replied Mrs. Jackson. "We're all going to help you."

"Me?" asked Vinnie.

"Yes, you," said Mrs. Jackson. "Vinnie, there are lots of young caregivers in this country. But there is help for them. And at this school, we're going to help you too."

"Thank you," said Vinnie.

"But there's one more e-mail," said Mrs. Jackson. "It's from a vacation company. Not one like Your Dream Vacation. A good one this time. They want to give you and your family a vacation to Florida."

"And it's free?" asked Vinnie.

"Yes," said Mrs. Jackson. "This time it's free."

Chapter 8

Just wow!

Vinnie had the ball. The goal was just in front of him, but there was someone between him and the goal. There was a girl from his team next to him.

"Vinnie, Vinnie! Kick it to me! Here! Here!" she shouted.

Vinnie looked at the girl. He quickly kicked the ball to her, and she kicked it into the goal.

"Goal!" shouted Vinnie. He and the girl jumped up and down happily.

"Well done, you two," said the coach. "That's a good play."

Vinnie smiled. "I love this vacation," he thought. All the kids were caregivers, and it was so easy to talk to them. Everybody felt like a friend. Next week he and his mother and his father were all going to Florida. And his father had a new job in New York.

"He's going to be living at home again," thought Vinnie. "It's wonderful. This is the best summer."

*   *   *

Two months later and it was a new year at school. For Vinnie, everything was different. His father was at home again, and his mother had a new caregiver. She came to their house in the morning and in the afternoon. She cleaned, she bought food from the store, and she made lunch for his mother too. Vinnie was on the school soccer team, and on Saturdays he and his father watched soccer on television.

Then, in October, Mrs. Jackson asked him to come to her office again.

"Hello, Vinnie," she said. "Come in. I want you to meet someone."

There was a tall man in Mrs. Jackson's office. He looked friendly.

"Hi, Vinnie," said the man. "My name is Peter, and I work for the New York Red Bulls."

"Wow," said Vinnie. "Really?"

"Yes," said Peter. "We do lots of work with organizations that help people in New York. And this year we're working with Young Caregivers. We're trying to help people like you, Vinnie."

"That's great," said Vinnie.

"But first we want you to help us," said Peter.

"Me?" asked Vinnie.

"Yes," said Peter. "We want our fans to give money to organizations like Young Caregivers. We need someone to tell our fans about their work. We need someone like you."

"But . . . how can I tell them?" said Vinnie. "I don't know many people."

"You can tell the fans about it at the game," said Peter. "On Saturday."

"Me?" asked Vinnie.

"Yes, you," said Peter. "And you can meet the Red Bulls team too."

"Me?" Vinnie asked again. "Meet the team?"

"Is that OK?" asked Peter. "Can you talk to the fans? Can you tell them about your work as a caregiver for your mother?"

Vinnie smiled. "Yes," he told Peter, "It's OK. I want to tell them everything."

"Great!" said Peter. He smiled too. "And this is for you and your friend, Tom."

He gave Vinnie an envelope.

*   *   *

"What?" shouted Tom. "Vinnie, say that again! You're going to meet the Red Bulls this Saturday?"

"Yes," laughed Vinnie, "and there's also this . . ."

He gave Tom the envelope. Tom opened it, and his eyes grew very big.

"It's a Red Bulls season ticket[14] for next year," Tom said.

"No," said Vinnie. "There are two Red Bulls season tickets. One is for you, and one is for me!"

"Wow!" said Tom.

"Yeah," said Vinnie. "Just wow!"

LOOKING BACK

1 Check your answers to *Looking forward* on page 33.

ACTIVITIES

2 Put the sentences in order.

1 Vinnie's mom says his friends need to know about her arthritis. ☐

2 Lots of people visit the school Web site. ☐

3 Vinnie's mom sees something is wrong with Vinnie. ⑴

4 Mrs. Jackson gives Vinnie a letter from Young Caregivers. ☐

5 Tom writes about Vinnie's mom on the school Web site. ☐

6 Vinnie and Tom get season tickets for the Red Bulls. ☐

7 Peter comes to Mrs. Jackson's office. ☐

8 A vacation company gives Vinnie and his parents a free vacation. ☐

3 Match the two parts of the sentences.

1 Why does Vinnie go to Mrs. Jackson's office? ⟨c⟩

2 Why does Lisa send Vinnie an e-mail? ☐

3 Why is Vinnie happier now? ☐

4 Why do Tom's eyes grow very big? ☐

5 What do Vinnie and his dad do on Saturdays? ☐

a Vinnie gives him a Red Bulls season ticket.

b She's a caregiver too.

c She wants to give him the e-mails and letters.

d They watch soccer on TV.

e His dad is at home again, and his mom has a new caregiver.

46

4 Are the sentences true (*T*) or false (*F*)?

1 Vinnie's mom and dad can pay for an expensive hotel. [F]
2 Zoe and her family have a lot of problems. ☐
3 Vinnie's friends are angry about the contest. ☐
4 Young Caregivers wants to give Vinnie's mom and dad a vacation. ☐
5 Vinnie's dad gets a new job in New York. ☐
6 Peter comes to Vinnie's classroom. ☐
7 Peter wants Vinnie to tell people about his work as a caregiver. ☐
8 There is one Red Bulls season ticket in the envelope. ☐

5 <u>Underline</u> the correct words in each sentence.

1 There are a lot of e-mails on Mrs. Jackson's *chair* / <u>*desk*</u>.
2 Lisa lives in *Florida* / *England*.
3 Vinnie *hates* / *likes* his vacation with Young Caregivers.
4 Vinnie is going to meet the *Galaxy* / *Red Bulls* team on Saturday.

6 Answer the questions.

1 What does Vinnie tell his friends at school?

....

2 How can everyone in the world read about Vinnie?

....

3 Where is Vinnie going to tell the Red Bulls fans about his mother?

....

47

GLOSSARY

• •

[1] **fan** (page 7) *noun*   someone who really likes a sports team

[2] **look after** (page 11) *verb*   try to make sure somebody is well

[3] **different** (page 12) *adjective*   not the same as somebody or something

[4] **contest** (page 14) *noun*   something a person tries to win

[5] **dream** (page 15) *adjective*   something you want very much

[6] **free** (page 16) *adjective*   when you don't need to give any money for something

[7] **hurt** (page 19) *verb*   when someone's body feels bad

[8] **office** (page 19) *noun*   a room where somebody works

[9] **downtown** (page 24) *noun*   in or to the central part of a city

[10] **winner** (page 28) *noun*   someone who wins a game or **contest**

[11] **pay** (page 30) *verb*   give money for something

[12] **caregiver** (page 33) *noun*   someone who **looks after** a person

[13] **organization** (page 40) *noun*   a group of people who work together to help other people

[14] **season ticket** (page 45) *noun*   a ticket you can use many times (e.g., to see a soccer game), but don't need to **pay** for each time